" What is a Mockbook™?"

Someone once said that laughter is the best medicine. We have taken that lesson to heart, done some soul searching and determined that our mission in life from this point on is to make others laugh. Studies have found that laughing boosts your immunity and can even help you recover from illness. Whether you are laughing with someone else or at yourself, all of your concerns and worries are forgotten – even if only for a few moments. Unfortunately, America seems to have lost its sense of humor lately. We are here to change that, in a very big way!

Our solution is the Mockbook. A Mockbook is a book without a story; no beginning, ending or confusing plot in between. A Mockbook can be placed on your bookshelf in mint condition – no scuffs, tears or folded pages to worry about. We guarantee that when visitors peruse your book collection, this is the only book they will be able to judge by its cover. And when they open it up and see the blank pages, a good laugh will follow!

We would be surprised if more than half the books that are sold on any given day are actually read after they are taken home. We don' t know anyone, with the exception of students, who has time to read anymore. There is just too much to do and not enough free time. In fact, a best-selling author recently remarked that he was a famous writer in a country where people don' t read. Fortunately for you, a Mockbook only takes a couple of minutes to read and will make you laugh out loud, thereby saving you time <u>and</u> improving your health.

Mockbooks also make great gifts for your family and friends. Just imagine their joy and laughter after opening the book and finding only blank pages staring back at them. Now that is truly priceless! As an incentive for helping us achieve our mission of laughter, use the order form on the next page and you will receive <u>10% off the entire order</u> when you buy three or more books.

<**WARNING**>: Laughter is contagious and this book will infect you.

Brook & Julie Syers

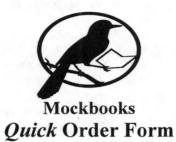

Mockbooks
Quick Order Form

**ORDER NOW AND GET <u>10% OFF THE ENTIRE ORDER</u>
WHEN YOU BUY 3 OR MORE BOOKS!!!**

Fax Orders: 419-281-6883. Send this form.

Telephone Orders: 800-247-6553. Have your
credit card ready.

Email Orders: order@bookmaster.com
Internet Orders: www.mockbooks.com

Postal Orders: Mockbooks, P.O. Box 388,
Ashland, OH 44805

Name: _____

Address: _____

City: _____ State:_____ Zip:_____

Telephone: _____ E-mail:_____

Sales Tax: Please add applicable sales tax for products shipped to Texas and Ohio addresses.

Payment: ☐ Check ☐ Credit Card:
☐ Visa ☐ MasterCard ☐ AMEX ☐ Discover

Card number: _____

Name on card: _____ Exp. Date:_____